This book Belongs to

_____

Cuss 'N' Color

Thank you for buying my color book!

Ever just have one of those days where you want to randomly shout swear words but resist because you are at work or surrounded by others and you can't behave inappropriately? We all do. Here's your chance to unwind and let a few choice words fly without anyone else knowing, unless you want to share, of course.

Here you will find a collection of vulgar words ranging from common to creative for you to color and unwind with. So go ahead, pick up a colored pencil, marker, crayon, or whatever strikes your fancy and create some extraordinary expletives.

This color book comes complete with adorable little animals (the perpetually happy little a$$holes.) Everyone knows there is no better way to say $#@& you, or *&$!%#@ %#$@ than a sweet baby bunny.

Have fun coloring and for anyone who says color books are only for kids...

&%#@ them.

Color Test Page

Test your colors here

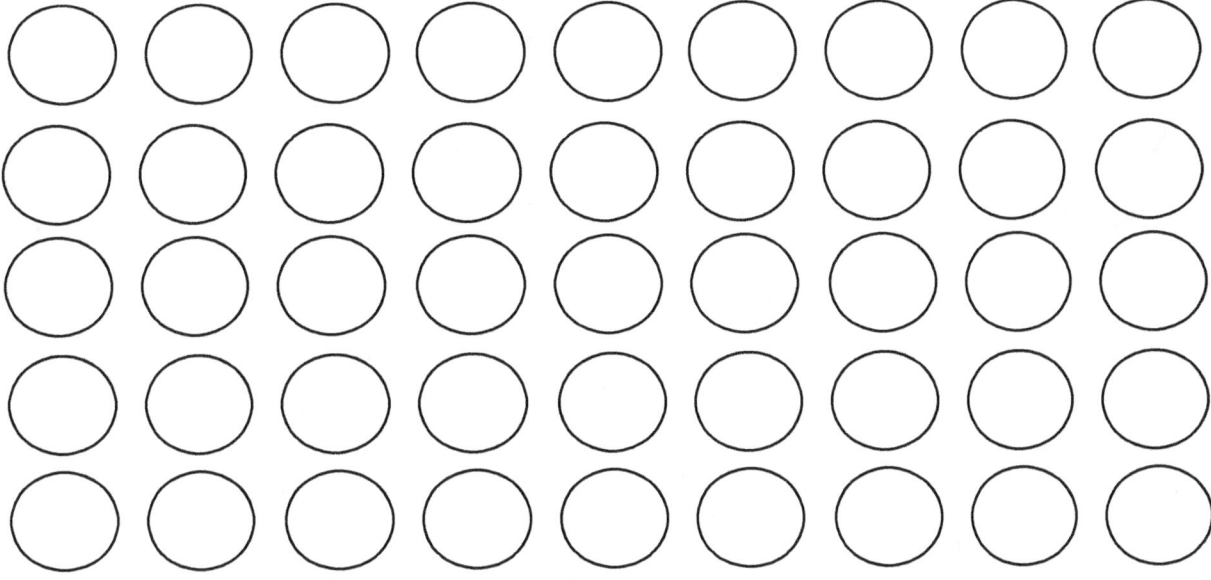

Cut out this page and insert behind the page you are currently coloring.

ASSGOBLIN

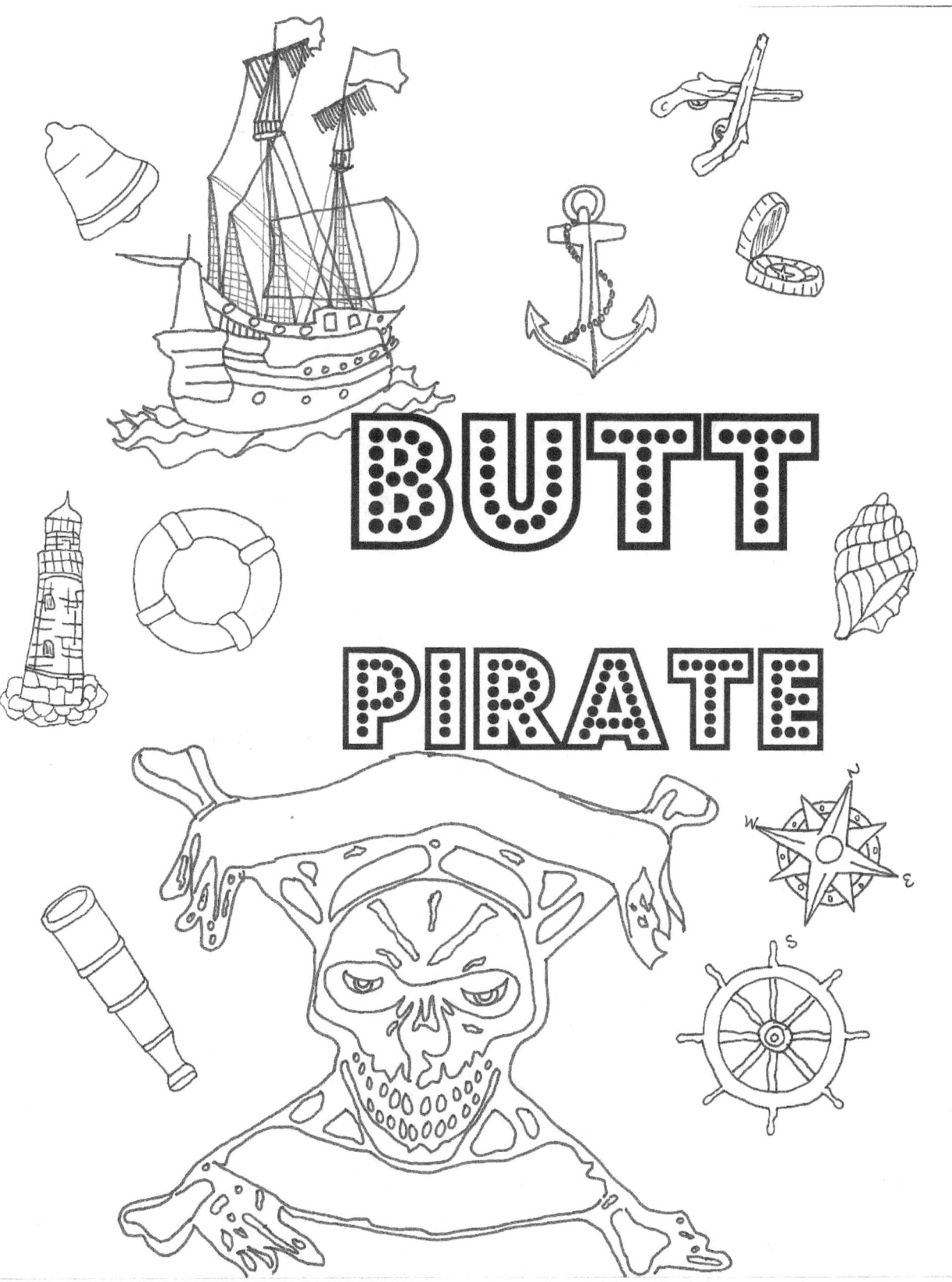

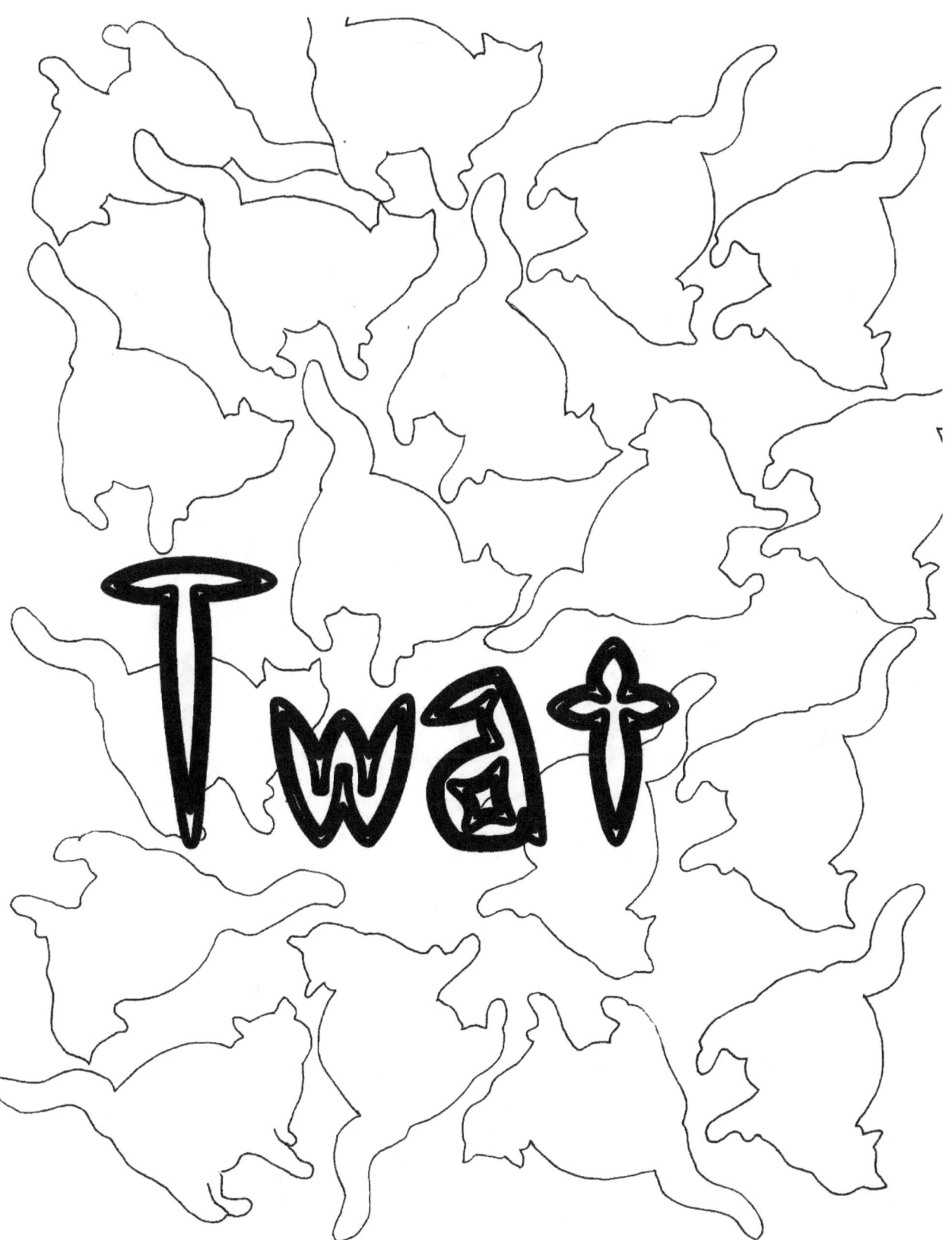

JERKOFF

Thanks
for buying my
Damn book, if
you like it,
please tell all
the other
assholes you
know by sharing

a fucking review on amazon. You are totally fucking amazing at being an artist, by the fucking way!